MOMENTUM ST(

I0036078

*Investing and Trading on the Stock Market Like a Genius by Analyzing
and Understanding the Trends*

Descrierea CIP a Bibliotecii Naționale a României

Momentum Stocks. Investing and Trading on the Stock Market Like a Genius by Analyzing and Understanding the Trends. – Bucharest: My Ebook, 2018
    ISBN 978-606-983-591-3

MOMENTUM STOCKS

Investing and Trading on the Stock Market Like a Genius by Analyzing and Understanding the Trends

INTRODUCTION

I want to thank you and congratulate you for buying the book, *"Momentum Stocks: Investing and Trading on the Stock Market Like a Genius by Analyzing and Understanding the Trends"*.

This book has actionable information on how to invest and trade on the stock market like a genius by analyzing and understanding the trends.

"The trend is your friend"

You've probably heard this saying before; of course it's one of the oldest sayings in the stock trading and investing world but what you might not know is that this saying is a shorter version of a longer sentence. The fuller version is actually *"The trend is your friend, until the end when it bends!"*

This full version affirms that there are two types of trend traders – those who follow the trend and make profits, and those who follow the trend, make profits and then lose it in the end.

Which of these traders do you want to be?

Trend trading is certainly a good thing – people like John. W. Henry earned millions of dollars from trend trading. From the proceeds of his investments, he bought the Boston Red Sox and the Liverpool Football Club and today, he is worth over $2.2billion.

The truth is that trend following is a very controversial topic; many financial advisors would advise you to stay off trend stocks, and that they don't work for stocks but people like John. W. Henry have proven them wrong.

People who tell you to stay off trend following simply have no idea about how to trade trend stocks; there are methods to these things, and in this book, you're about to learn some of the secret strategies that successful trend traders use.

You're going to learn:

- What trend following is
- Where to find the best trend stocks
- When to buy a stock
- When to take your profits
- When to exit a losing trade

And basically everything you need to know about profiting from momentum stocks without getting wiped out.

This book is beginner friendly as it is suitable for experienced traders who need to master the trend trading game. Let's begin.

Thanks again for buying this book. I hope you enjoy it!

Respective authors own all copyrights not held by the publisher.

The information herein is offered for informational purposes solely, and is universal as so. The presentation of the information is without contract or any type of guarantee assurance.

The trademarks that are used are without any consent, and the publication of the trademark is without permission or backing by the trademark owner. All trademarks and brands within this book are for clarifying purposes only and are the owned by the owners themselves, not affiliated with this document.

TABLE OF CONTENTS

Introduction 5

Chapter 1: Introduction to Trend Trading 11

    What is an Uptrend? 11
    What's a Downtrend? 13

Chapter 2: How to Find and Identify Momentum Stocks 16

    Where to Find Momentum Stocks 17

Chapter 3: When to Buy Momentum Stocks 20

Chapter 4: When to Sell Momentum Stocks 25

Chapter 5: Risk Management Strategies-How to Keep Your Shirt When Everyone is Losing Theirs 28

Chapter 6: How to Profit from Short Selling Your Momentum Stocks 32

Conclusion 37

Before we discuss the hows of trend trading, we will start by building a strong understanding of what trend trading is all about.

Chapter 1: *Introduction to Trend Trading*

Putting it simply, a momentum stock is a stock that has been moving in a certain direction for a long period of time. A momentum stock could be moving in an uptrend or a downward trend.

What is an Uptrend?

An uptrend is a chart with consistently higher lows. This happens when there is a pullback in the price of a stock, and traders decide that the period when stock prices are falling is the perfect time to purchase the stock.

As many traders continue to purchase the stock, the increase in buying rates adds more demand to the market, and the stock commands a higher price.

This increase in stock price would show on the chart as an upward movement. This is what is called an uptrend is stock trading.

Let's put the technical jargon aside and bring it close to home; So your co-worker Janet sees some really nice shoes in a store for $35. This same shoes were selling for $50 the last time you bought visited the boutique. Now, it's selling for $35 – probably because it's Black Friday, or because the store wants to clear out its stocks.

For whatever reason, the shoes are selling for way cheaper than its value so when Janet comes back to the office with those shoes and informs you and the others of the new price, you all decide that it's a steal.

So you and four other co-workers rush to grab your own shoes. You get home and tell your neighbors, and every single one of your co-workers who bought the shoes tells their friends, neighbors, siblings and church members of how the latest shoes in town are selling for 15% less than its original price.

So everyone keeps rushing down to the store to grab their own shoes.

But you know what they say about demand and supply? The higher the demand, the higher the price goes.

So the store gets wind of what is happening – many people are buying this shoe so they increase the price to $40.

People still keep trooping in to buy the shoe because it's still a bargain at $40 since it sells for $50 or more in other places.

At $40, people are still trooping in to purchase the shoes so the store increases the price to $45. Of course, it's still cheaper than it sells in other places, and for its value so people are still trooping in to purchase this cheap shoe.

Many of these people are coming to buy this shoe at cheap rates because they plan to resell it when the store runs out of stock, ends the promo, or decides to return the prices back to the original price.

This is exactly how an uptrend occurs in the stock market. As seen in the graph below, the stock prices will continue to rise as there is an increase in demand for the stocks in the market.

What's a Downtrend?

A downtrend is simply the opposite of an uptrend. A downtrend is a series of lower highs.

This happens when traders are deciding that a stock is no longer worth holding and they start selling their stocks. At this point, the sellers are actually willing to agree to sell their stocks at prices that are lower just so that they can dispose of their stocks.

The increased level of sales puts a pressure on the market and forces the prices down. If you remember your demand and supply laws well, you will remember that an increase in supply will always force prices down.

So this is exactly what happens in a downtrend – sellers dump their stocks in the market and this forces the prices of the stocks to go lower.

Each attempt that the particular stock tries to make to increase in price only ends up with a price that is much lower before the stock price can get as high as the previous stock price.

So what is Momentum Stocks Trading?

Momentum stock trading involves taking advantage of upward trends in the stock market to make profits for yourself – you will enter into a position when the stock is trading in an upward direction, and hold your position until a specific timeframe, which is usually before the trend starts to reverse.

So basically, you want to be able to hold your shirt when everyone is losing theirs – you want to be able to make profits even when the market is in a free fall.

A practical example of momentum stock trading can be seen in the case of the dotcom stocks; those were momentum stocks.

Between the late 90's and the early 2000's, stocks like Cisco, Yahoo, Oracle, and EBay were on an upward trend. Many people bought them and saw their portfolios grow rapidly.

Sadly, most of these people lost out when the markets began to crash.

This is why you need to keep the number one rule for momentum stocks trading in mind "*Never use a buy and hold strategy for trading momentum stocks*".

Those who lost out during the dotcom era were mostly 'buy and hold' investors who believed that the stocks were going to continue to maintain their upward trend. Momentum stocks are highly volatile so to trade them, you have to know how to get in and out very quickly.

Trend trading has been around for hundreds of years even before the dotcom stocks and will continue for years. Most humans are driven by greed and fear – and this is what makes momentum stock trading a sweet strategy – people rush to buy stocks when the prices are rising, and they rush to sell them whenever they fear that the stocks prices will drop. In other words, fear and greed is what drives stocks on an upward and downward trend and your job now would be to learn how to identify momentum stocks without being greedy, and know when to sell them off without being driven by fear. Those who make crazy money out of this just have to find their sweet spot!

In the next chapter, you'll learn how to find and identify momentum stocks.

Chapter 2: How to Find and Identify Momentum Stocks

As a momentum stock trader, your end game is different from an equity investor-you are not a very patient trader. Equity traders look for reasonably priced stocks, buy them, and then hold them for a very long time until the inherent risks have reduced and the stocks have become stable so that they can sell them at profitable rates.

Fine, that's a nice strategy but as a momentum trader, you're looking for stocks that are hot on the market – that will make you profits at short, regular intervals.

You're looking for stocks that have the potential to soar in prices within a short holding period.

These stocks would usually not remain in their position for a long period of time but by the time they start losing their values, you would have made your profits.

This is like the 'quickie' of stock trading.

So where can you find, and how do you identify these stocks?

Where to Find Momentum Stocks

When trading momentum stocks, you don't look for stocks of slow-growing companies-companies with 1% annual growth rate or market caps of several billions of dollars. It would take a lot of money flowing in to move such stocks.

For instance, General Electric has a market cap of about $271billon, and its annual growth rate is around 1% every year. General Electric does not qualify as a good momentum stock because its future earnings are easy to predict and like I said earlier, it would take a lot of money flowing in to move the market.

But let's compare it to a smaller market like Tesla, with a $30 Billion current market Cap. Tesla is relatively new on the scene and its future earnings and revenues are not easy to predict so the stock prices are volatile and every dollar that flows in would have roughly 10 times more effect than General Electric because it has a smaller relative float. Tesla is a great momentum stock because you can easily ride on the waves to make some profits for yourself.

To make money from momentum stocks, you have to look for companies that meet these two basic criteria:

1: New Technology Companies

Yes, companies like Tesla that are inventing new things or making new technologies popular. Look for new companies in the high-tech industries making new innovations in the information technology, software, engineering, and biotechnology industry.

Because they are creating new markets and disrupting the status quo, these companies are usually able to grow rapidly. However, there are no guarantees that they would continue to increase – Apple was once a momentum stock when it came with its innovative smart phones and gadgets. Cisco, Microsoft and Oracle were also momentum stocks at some point but right now, they are now dividend-paying stalwarts. Stocks that pay dividends are usually not suitable for trend trading.

2: New Formula Companies

Imagine a company like McDonald's, Panera Bread, Home Depot, Tractor Supply or Starbucks that came with new formulas that shook the market. These are also great momentum stocks because they have very high growth and sales potentials.

Even though they would eventually saturate their markets and become dividend-paying stocks like McDonald's is right now, you are guaranteed of high company growth rates, and rapid revenue growths at least during that period when the inventions made by these companies are moving and shaking the market.

So basically, you're looking for companies with high revenue growth rates. Companies like Apple that grew its revenues between 29% and 79% annually between 2005 and 2012 until 2013 when revenue growth rates slowed down to 9%, and then 7% in 2014 and since then it has been single digit revenue growth rates.

Or companies like Chipotle. Chipotle was also a new formula company and it experienced a double digit annual revenue growth rate between 2005 and 2014. Chipotle had a 31% revenue growth rate in 2006.

So in summary, as a trend trader, you're looking to buy:

- Stocks of New Formula or New Technology Companies with an annual revenue growth rate of at least 20% or more. Good momentum stocks will often have higher revenue growth rates in their early years. You can see growth rates of 30%, 50% or more than 100%. These are ideal candidates for momentum stocks.

Next, we will be discussing where to buy momentum stocks.

Chapter 3: **When to Buy Momentum Stocks**

You already know the types of companies whose stocks you should be looking to buy as they qualify as momentum stocks.

However, you can't just go ahead and buy them; you have to watch and wait until the market says you can go ahead and buy them – you have to wait for the right market indicators.

Remember that momentum trend trading isn't just about buying stocks with high annual revenue growth rates, but stocks whose stock prices are going up.

If the stocks are not moving on an upward trend, you have no business buying them, or speculating on them. You want to buy only stocks that have showed momentum.

So when do you buy the stocks of these New Formula/New Technology companies that we have identified?

Buy when the stock's 50-day moving average closes higher than its 200-day moving average, and only if the stock is trading above its 50-day moving average when the crossover occurs.

This is the perfect time to buy momentum stocks.

So how do you calculate the 50-day or 200-day moving averages?

Moving Averages (MA) is an indicator in stock trading that helps to mathematically gauge the direction of a current trend to see if they are moving in an upward or downward trend.

It takes the closing prices of a stock over a period of time, adds it up, and divides it by the number of period.

So if I want to see the 10-day moving average of a stock, I will take the closing prices of those stocks over the past 10 days, and divide this by 10.

Let's have a practical example.

Let's say we have a company called Dalton Technology with closing rates as seen in the table below:

Date	Closing Rates
28/05/2017	$10.97
29/05/2017	$10.80
30/05/2017	$11.02
31/05/2017	$11.03
01/06/2017	$10.99
02/06/2017	$10.99
03/06/2017	$11.00
04/06/2017	$10.99
05/06/2017	$11.00
06/06/2017	$11.00

So we take the values for the 10 days and add it up (10.97+10.80+11.02+11.03......................... and so on until you have added up the values for the 10-day period).

That's gives us 98.8. Now we have to divide 98.8 by the number of days, which is 10 days.

So the 10-day moving average would be 98.8/10 = $9.88

So to find out the perfect time to buy your momentum stocks, you have to look at the company's closing prices over the past 50 days, and then over the past 200 days and calculate the moving average just like we did above.

You don't have to do a manual calculation as done above; there are a lot of online calculators that you can use to calculate moving averages for stocks.

Once the moving averages are calculated, they are plotted on a graph and then connected to create a moving average line.

It's possible to plot more than one moving average on a graph so a 50-moving average, and a 200-day moving average can be plotted on the same graph to enable you see when a stock's 50-day moving average closes higher than its 200-day moving average.

This is what is known as the GOLDEN CROSS.

Golden Cross

200 day MA

50 day MA

50day MA crosses above 200day MA signaling a change in momentum

The blue line above signifies the 50 day moving average, and the red line is the 200 day moving average.

So when the 50-day moving average cuts through the 200-day moving average, it shows that the stock is on an upward trend and you can expect that the stock prices will continue to rise – it signifies a change in momentum and it is mostly at this point that a stock qualifies to be called a momentum stock.

The second condition is that the stock has to be trading above its 50-day moving average.

So if the stock traded at $10 on day 50, you can buy on day 51 if the stock trades at a higher value than $10 when the crossover occurs.

This is a very simple indicator but it an extremely powerful one. Most of the greatest momentum stocks in history began their upward trend at this crossover stage so you can rely on it to show you where the money's at.

Let's now get to this next important topic – when to sell your momentum stocks.

Chapter 4: **When to Sell Momentum Stocks**

This is another important part to pay attention to because this is the part where you will either make profits or lose your investments.

There are three signals you should look out for:

1. The Death Cross

This simply refers to the opposite of the Golden Cross we talked about in the last chapter. It arises when the 50-day moving average actually closes right below the 200-day moving average.

As soon as this happens, it means that the trend is over and if you continue to hold on to the stocks, you may lose out in the end.

This is the best time to start taking out your profits, and you should sell your stocks at the open of market the next day.

Of course, you have to continue to keep your eyes the charts so that you can easily see when the death cross happens.

2. 300% Profit Margin

Another suitable time to take out your profits from momentum stocks is when the stock prices rise 300% above your entry price.

A lot of momentum stocks go on to rally around 200% profits while some momentum stocks crash almost immediately but from experience, a 300% move is the best spot to capture a good part of the uptrend and keep some profits for yourself without getting too greedy or getting burned out in the end.

Remember that:

"In stock trading, especially momentum stock trading, it's not about whether you are right or wrong but about the money you make when you're right, and how much you lose when you're wrong."

You don't have the time or resources to wait and see if your guesswork will pay off in the end, or if the market will crash the next day or otherwise so it's better to cash out when your investments have seen a significant growth rate than to continue to wait endlessly until the entire stocks crash rapidly.

It's possible that after you cash out, the stock prices may continue to grow and even grow to about 400% -500% or more but you still wouldn't be losing out because it's still a long way from your initial investment, and you're still going to earn good profits.

3. 15% Stop Loss

Another signal to exit a position is when the stock falls below 15% of your entry price. This is an emergency stop loss technique and even though you're not really making profits, it will help you avoid making too many losses.

Usually, a stock will not fall this much at the beginning of an uptrend so if you start to see a 15% drop in stock process, it's time to exit your position.

A 15% stop loss may seem wide but this is because of the volatile nature of momentum stocks – they tend to rise and fall in value so much that daily moves of above 5% are not unusual so for momentum stocks, it's always better to leave a wider stop loss margin so that you wouldn't be exiting your position out of panic, thereby throwing good profits out of the door.

A good stop loss margin would help you avoid panic selling so that you would only be selling when there's real danger lurking around.

Now let's talk about how to manage risks and prevent losses when investing in momentum stocks.

Chapter 5: Risk Management Strategies-How to Keep Your Shirt When Everyone is Losing Theirs

Now let's say you find this nice new technology company that has been growing its revenues north of 20% for about 2-3 years now, and you place it on your momentum stocks watch list and then a few months later, the golden cross happens – the 50-day moving average of the stock closes over its 200-day moving average and the stock is selling higher than its 50-day moving average.

Let's say the closing price of your momentum stock on the day the golden cross happens is \$18.07, the 50-day moving average is \$17.13, and the 200-day moving average is \$17.07.

And let's assume that you have about \$10,000 in your account to trade with, and you want to risk 2% of your account on each trade. So you have to first calculate the number of stocks you can buy as follows:

No. of shares to purchase = <u>size of account X percentage risked on trade</u>

Entry price – stop loss

But first, you have to calculate your stop loss price. Remember that in the last chapter we talked about how a 15% stop loss was the most appropriate margin to give for momentum stocks so to calculate your stop loss, you have to divide the current rate of the stock by 85% (100%-15%=85%).

The current rate of the stock is $18.07 so:

Stop loss= $18.07 x 0.85

= $15.36

Now you have to calculate the number of shares you want to buy as follows:

$$\frac{10,000 \text{ X } 2\%}{\$18.07 - \$15.36}$$

= 200/2.71

= 73.8 shares

This means that you can buy 74 shares so on the day after the golden cross happens, you purchase 74 shares but since the stock price would have gone up by that time, let's assume that you would be able to purchase them at around $18.11.

So on that day, you enter the market with 74 shares at an opening price of $18.11.

Due to the slight difference in entry price, you have to recalculate your stop loss.

Assuming you got your stocks at $18.11 per unit, your actual stop loss will be:

= $18.11 X 0.85

= $15. 39

Therefore, you have to set the emergency stop loss on your account to $15.39, and now you have to set your sell limit order.

You have to set your sell limit order to 300% above your entry price so that you can cash out when your stocks have gathered a lot of profits.

To calculate your 300% sell limit, you simply have to multiply your entry price by 4, which would be:

= $18.11 X 4

= $72.44

So when your stocks reach the $72.44 mark, you sell your stocks and you cash out.

Therefore, you set your emergency stop loss to $15.39 and your sell limit order to $72.44, and you do nothing – yes, you sit back and watch.

Remember that as a momentum stock trader, you are neither bearish nor bullish – just out there to take advantage of some stocks doing well, cash out, and earn good money so don't start hanging message boards, or obsessing over your stocks.

Set your limits and look out for your profits but you can use a 'Good till cancelled' limit order so that if for any reason you decide to exit your position earlier, you can easily do that.

The only thing you need to do is to check your moving averages every evening to see if the 50-day moving average crosses below the 200-day moving average so that you can take out your profits immediately before things start spiraling downwards.

But let's say in about six months, the stock prices rise to 300% and your sell limit order is fulfilled, you end up selling at $72.44. If you deduct this from your entry price of $18.11, that means you captured about $54.33 points from just one stock.

Multiply that by the number of shares you bought (54.33 X 74 shares), that's a whooping profit of about $4,020, and a return on interest of more than 40% in an account worth $10,000 and considering you only risked 2% of your account on this trade, that's an impressive return on investment.

Let's say you were a more aggressive trader, and instead of 20%, you risked 10%, you would have made a 200% return on interest but you shouldn't do that.

Rather than risk 10% on one momentum stock, it helps to look for about 10-15 momentum stocks, and invest 2% of your account on each stock.

This way, your profit potentials will increase, and since you already have a clever strategy for reducing losses, you won't have to lose a lot of money even when things don't turn out as expected. Next, we will be talking about profits.

Chapter 6: How to Profit from Short Selling Your Momentum Stocks

In the last chapter, we talked about how to profit from holding a long position on momentum stocks, where you have to wait until the stocks grow to about 300% before you cash out.

However, with momentum stocks, you can't always wait that long – sometimes, you may have to take advantage of the short term spikes in stock values to earn some quick profits.

The good thing about trend trading is that you're not there to predict the market; you're there to ride on the trend.

You can't predict what will happen in the future but you sure can take advantage of what is unfolding before your eyes.

Every bear market begins when the death cross happens – when the 50-day moving average crosses below the 200-day moving average. It may be impossible to predict a bear market but you can avoid getting caught up in one by exiting a long position as soon as the death cross occurs.

Like I mentioned earlier, momentum stocks are highly volatile and they can go up several percentages within an hour just like they can go down several percentages within hours too.

It's not impossible to see a stock that had been trading upwards of $20 for the past 3 years crash to around $10 within six (6) months or less. The truth is that momentum stocks end up giving up most, if not all of their growth after a period. In the past, bear markets like the dotcom bear market, we saw stocks decline to about 90% from their highs.

This happens because towards the end of an uptrend, the stocks start trading at irrational prices such that no business revenues or growth would be able to justify such earnings multiples.

During the uptrend, no one is thinking about this; everyone is focused on how to make money from the uptrend. However, when the downtrend begins, you'll see many investors brining out their calculators to assess the multiples and that's when they realize how crazy the market has gone, so they start dumping their stocks because they are now able to see that there's no way the market will be able to hold up for a long time.

The quick reversal and downward spiral of the uptrend is usually triggered by this realization.

Shorting momentum stocks is a good idea at this point because you can make decent profits from it; however, it can be a highly risky move and should be done with utmost care.

- **Rule 1**: Don't short momentum stocks on the way up; you should only short your stocks after the death cross occurs.
- **Rule 2**: Search for stocks with massive run-ups but a reverse growth that is beginning to slow down.

So to short momentum stocks, make sure the stocks are available to be borrowed from your stock broker and set a 'sell short' order on your account.

Then at the end of the trade, use a 'buy to cover' order to buy back the shares and return them to your broker.

Since you bought low and sold high, you would have made money because the stock would have declined in value by the time you're trying to buy back and the one you borrowed from your stock broker would have been sold at a higher rate.

Let's have a practical example now, let's say you got 100 units from your broker when the stocks were selling at $5.40, and you sell short, you would sell at $540.

The stock is on a downward trend now so by the next day, or the next 7 days, the stocks may have dropped to around $5.10. This is when you execute your buy to cover order and buy back the 100 units you borrowed from your broker.

So you spend $510 buying back the stocks and at the end of the day, you're able to keep $30 for yourself. This doesn't look like much but when you consider larger trades worth thousands of units, you can easily make impressive profits from short selling.

However, if it turns out that the stock has gone up at the time when you want to buy it back, you will lose money.

This is why you must adhere to the rules I mentioned above:

- Short sell only when the death cross has occurred.
- Short sell only stocks with massive run-ups
- Short sell only stocks with dwindling growth rates

The market is quick to punish such companies so your chances of making a winning with stocks like this are somewhat guaranteed.

Also, keep in mind that the best time to short sell stocks is when the momentum has reversed sharply – never before.

Another point to note is that when you will be expected to pay a fee on the stocks borrowed from your broker.

Usually, when the downward trend begins, the brokers place those stocks on their hard to borrow list so it becomes much more expensive to borrow them.

Some brokers may have you pay as much as 100% annualized so if the shorted stock drops to zero within a year, you need to pay your broker 100% interests because you held the stocks at 100% annualized borrow rate.

This is why it is very important to time your short selling so that even if you borrow stocks at a 100% annualized rate, you can still earn 50% on shorting the stocks within 3 months and then you refund borrowing costs of 25% to your broker to cover the three month period.

You will still have a net return of around 25% to keep to yourself.

CONCLUSION

We have come to the end of the book. Thank you for reading and congratulations for reading until the end.

While it is very much possible to short sell momentum stocks and earn short-term profits, it's best to leave that strategy for experienced traders only.

When you're starting out, start with holding long positions so that you can avoid the risks and complications of short-selling and still make good profits for yourself and when the bear market begins, you can get your cards off the table, profit in hand and take a trip to somewhere nice to enjoy the proceeds of your hard work.

If you found the book valuable, can you recommend it to others? One way to do that is to post a review on Amazon.

Click here to leave a review for this book on Amazon!

Thank you and good luck!

www.ingramcontent.com/pod-product-compliance
Lightning Source LLC
Chambersburg PA
CBHW071126210326
41519CB00020B/6443